An Amusing Alphabet

Written and illustrated by

Irene Wittig

For Rachel, Ben, Cyrus, and Lorna

Annabel and Andrew ate apples
under the arbor
one April afternoon

Aa

The bears baked buns, bread and birthday cakes in Bruno's Bakery

Can you also find the bundt cake, big buildings and the color blue?

Bb

Cassandra Cat checks the cash as Calvin Clown chats with Cornelius Crocodile

Can you also find the cashier's cabin, the clown, and the canopy?

Cc

Cashier

Dinosaur and Dragon dine at the deli
down by the docks

*Can you also find the ducks, the dogs, the door,
the hot dog, and the doughnuts?*

Dd

The elephants paint Easter eggs
before eleven

*Can you also find the earth, the eagle,
the elephant's eyes, and his eyeglasses?*

Ee

Freddy Fox forgot his fishing basket

Can you also find the flowers,
the fern, the fish and the feather?

Ff

Greta Gopher grows gladiolas
in her garden

*Can you also find the grasshopper
and the color green?*

Gg

Harry and Henrietta Hog hover by the haunted house on Halloween

Can you also find the hat?

Hh

Inspector Impala inquires
where the ill eagle is

He's inside!

Ii

Jake Jackal drives by the jonquils
in his jaunty jalopy

Jj

Kangaroos and koalas in kindergarten

*Can you also find the koala kicking the ball
and the knapsack?
(That's a hard one because the K is silent!)*

Kk

Leonard Lion brought his lute and lilies
to the lovely Lisa

Can you tell that Lisa is a lioness?

Ll

Mr. and Mrs. Moth get married
in the merry month of May

Mm

Nick and Nora Newt in New York

*Is it **n**ighttime?*
No.

Nn

An outstanding orchestra at the Oasis Café

Can you also find the orangutan and her ocarina,
the octopus' one-man-band,
and the organ, the ox, and the ocelot?

Oo

Penguin, parrot, peacock, pelican and puffin pose for portraits

*Can you also find the perch,
the potted plant, and the photographer?*

Pp

Quincy Quail sits quietly
on the queen's quilt

Did he jump on quickly?

Qq

Rugged Ranger Rat rides on the range

*Can you also find the rope
and the color red?*

Rr

Seymour Snake sips a soda
in the summer sun

Can you also find the sand, the straw, the sunglasses, the stripes, and the little sombrero?

Ss

Timothy Tiger tends to
the train travelers' tickets

*Can you also find the trolley, the trunk, the turtle,
the teddy bear, tapir, toucan, toad, and tuna,
and the trees, town, and tower?*

Tt

Unique Unicorn in uniform

He's unusual but not at all ugly

Uu

Vivien Vicuna visits Dr. Vandervulture, the veterinarian

Can you also find the violets, vitamins, vial and v-chart?

Vv

Wallaby and Weasel wash windows
with the wise Wizard

Can you also find the walrus and his wand?

Ww

The young Yak and the zany Zebra play the xylophone with zest

Xx,Yy,Zz

Remember to practice your ABCs

M   N   O   P

Q   R   S   T

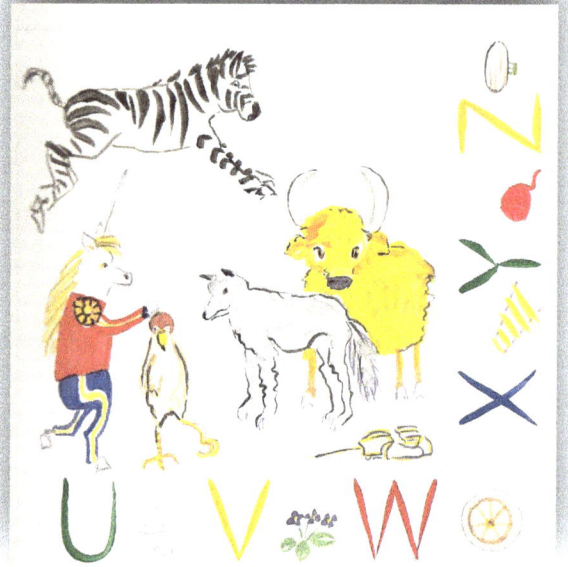

U   V   W   X   Y   Z

The Alphabet Menagerie

www.ingramcontent.com/pod-product-compliance
Lightning Source LLC
Chambersburg PA
CBHW040248100426

42811CB00011B/1191